Groundcover

Molly Kugel

Tolsun Books
Flagstaff, Arizona

for my parents

Contents

I. *dry garden*

Herbarium — 2
Bereaved — 4
Toward Them — 6
Groundcover — 8
lily, dahlia, gladiolus, daffodil — 10

II. *spring and summer*

Shape of Iris — 12
The Forest of the Suburbs — 14
bluebell, harebell, witch's thimble — 15
Protected by a Spine — 16
Wangari Muta Maathai — 18
Ghost needle weld — 19
Anna Atkins — 21
Afterlives — 23
Boy, Age 7 — 24
Mid-century Modern Sofa — 25
Sepal — 27
History of Shell — 28
The Skin of Willow Bark — 30
Dear One — 32

III. *fall and winter*

Nicatiana tabacum — 34
Annie Darwin's Writing Box — 36
Condolences — 37
Leningrad, 1938 — 39
Kitchen Ghosts — 40
Leaf, moon, stone — 41
Dental Records — 42
Dickinson walking through the woods — 43

Lancaster, A Fragment   45
Linnet   46
Lady algologist   47
Penn's Woods   48
Recordings   49

IV. spring and summer

April 1977   52
The Wave Machine in Oliver's Room   53
Incantations   54
Home Studies in Nature   56
Forsythia   58
Understory   59
Persephone   60
Late August   62
Cashel   64
Jane Colden below the guardrail   65
The Wave Machine in Ingrid's Room   67
Ghost pipe, ghost plant, corpse plant
    (1886 and backwards)   69
Ghost pipe, ghost plant, corpse plant
    (1886 and before)   70
Taraxacum   71
Ghost garden   72
Lantana   73
Herbarium   75
Culling Stone   76
Moss   77
Diatoms   79
petrichor   81

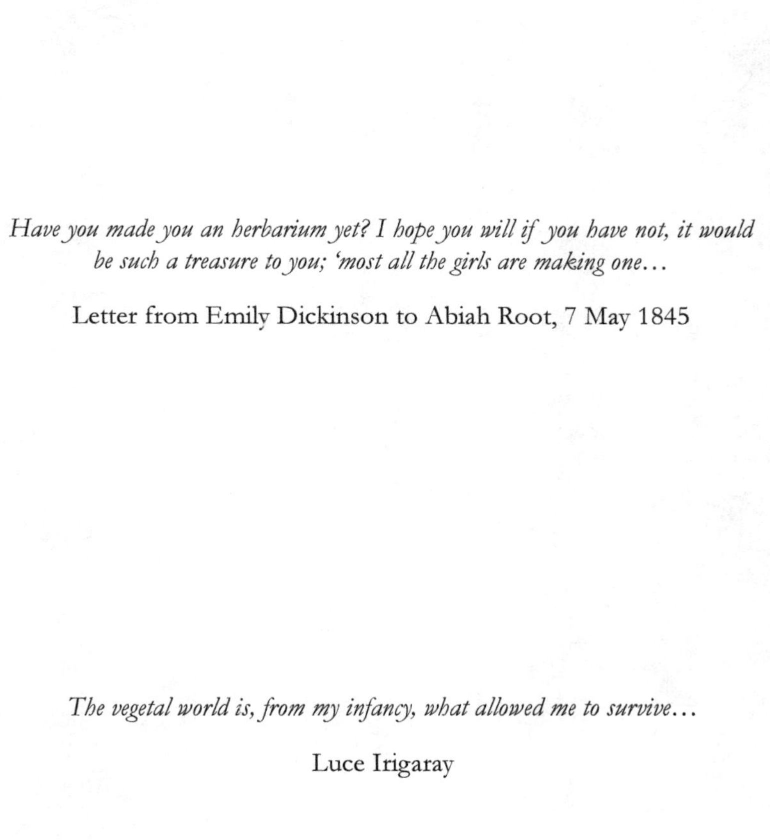

Have you made you an herbarium yet? I hope you will if you have not, it would be such a treasure to you; 'most all the girls are making one…

Letter from Emily Dickinson to Abiah Root, 7 May 1845

The vegetal world is, from my infancy, what allowed me to survive…

Luce Irigaray

I. dry garden

Herbarium

Why do you keep returning,
revenant, reckless, and barefoot?
It is green and the greenest.

It is a good thing tried hard,
something other people doubted
of you, or a child's last call to his mother,

but this time she knows the way.
It is near again.
It is all the lost things:

the flower bracelet for your birthday,
dropped by the main line train station,
first dances on gravel, car radios

and open car doors and starlight
and moon's light and light, dying and tender.
Look, everything is glowing:

the pachysandra, grape hyacinth,
leaves of the maple tree you had trouble
climbing, and your mother will call you

for dinner soon, but for now
the backyard is quiet and your knees
are young and it will be summer now.

No one will question where the years
have gone—no one will
know the difference.

Herbarium, Lancaster, 1977, 1980, 1990, Ardmore, 2013

Bereaved

*The third feature of the post-pastoral is the recognition that the inner is also
the workings of the outer, that our inner human nature can be understood in
relation to external nature.* –Terry Gifford

Please understand that you aren't unique—
these feelings, none of this original,

common as the American crow,
slighter than the raven, more foreboding than the blackbird.

Mourning arrests us on a rocky path or the sandy one
you remember near the dunes—it informs us

to go outside into the open clearing,
between the twisted willow—

here we walk near our dead,
passing them without salutations.

On a few branches, artifacts shiver in the wind,
a knitted scarf, a knotted necktie.

Who can say for certain if they are there or aren't there,
but we see tremendous flocks, brown eyes, black feathers,

a sheen of iridescence, purple or blue, tenacity of flight—
the attempts at extermination with dynamite in our country

failed terribly, the crow prevailing like that pang in your chest,
how deep the hollowing, a cavern near your ribs, as far as

the depths of Orpheus' journey to the underworld;
it is a kind of hope to think we can bring them back,

as though the natural world bends its rules or could even
cower to save itself against the fire and flood of us.

The crows follow the rules, or we assume as much,
classify it a "crow funeral" when they all gather round

a fallen body, but naturalists say
it is also reconnaissance:

measuring danger, checking
for a pulse, searching for a reason.

Then after,
it is like closing your eyes.

Toward Them

In the meantime, as the world is burning,
before the brink of extinction,
we must take stock.

Ten bushes of *Asclepias tuberosa*, butterfly a-flying-weed,
a citrus-colored singing, an aria along the roadside,
prefer glades and prairies born from rain shadow.

Oh forb, coarse perennial, milkweed-one,
near the longleaf pine habitat, burned
for restoration—you, pleurisy, yearn

for open air, a broken canopy,
and grow in the wake of controlled burn,
seem to thrive when we comb you and try to understand.

Named for what you would kill
or cure—a tea steeped with skunk cabbage
for that pain in the chest,

a hard breath—some colonists later considered you
a panacea after learning
botany from the Menominee people

but instead of truth they learned use:
there wasn't a tobacco offering; there wasn't any singing
to your roots as they dug in a meadow of quiet,

a songless air, hushed and torn radix.
They possessed you like brocades, damask, or scarlet shoes,
used you for flu, colds, fever, diarrhea, nausea
                    and assorted pulmonary issues.

Was there once a chance to evolve:
the ecstasy of an herbarium,
the euphoria of Thoreau walking clubs?

Learn the names again, say the Latin
from Asclepius, Greek god of healing,
the medicinal, something sacred, *sacren* the obsolete

twelfth-century verb "to make holy" or the Old French
sacrer "to consecrate, anoint, dedicate," another
act of dominion—it seems to all lead back to this place.

There were those who told us what to love,
who told us of this approach, this encroaching
grief upon our shoulder.

Even at this late hour,
all long asleep, covered in sheets,
we could still wander out to a glen,

near a pine wood;
their orange stars will open one by one—
let's make our way toward them.

Groundcover

The ground doesn't belong to you but is also yours
in that it's made of your body—
your cells, your pulsing, the things you're remembering

now about your mother folding laundry in the hallway
as you drifted to sleep amidst that dim light.
Perennial, glow-gray, silky-lanate hairs,

so wooly, antispasmodic,
named *wooly woundwort*,
as wound dressing, poultice, antiseptic.

These carpet below, hold the buttoned mass of us.
They're a way to stem bleeding, analgesic,
eared-leaves, wrinkling warm,

not listening, ear-to-ear, the flowers,
sessile, without petiole, closest to the stem.
No distance of a leafstalk to grow away from harm.

We have to come closer.
The cold silver bundles together.
The root is felt by the stem and by the leaf, felt.

Like what a family won't say about death.
To stem, to stanch, to hide one with another.
We follow and are undetected.

Internally, we could steep it
in a tea for fevers, hemorrhaging,
a hidden, inhibited clotting,

weakness of the liver and heart.
Above ground we bend back
into alabaster *stachys byzantina.*

The lamb's ear holds us
for a little while.

operculum terra, Lancaster, 1977

(9)

lily, dahlia, gladiolus, daffodil

Kneel by the dirt, measure two or three
times as deep as the bulb is tall.
This is the digging, the planting of bulbs and bulbils—
the nose is up and the roots are down.
There is a vulnerability in having been seen before,
before the bloom, as though dormant now,
as though held quiet, as though you were ever
truly seen when you were only a body unable to move,
a short stem with scales, food stores,
a way to survive underground through wintering.
Like a hatchling before hatching, there is hope
in the invisible—there is hope in a kind of leafing return.

And then the opposite is true.
How is it to be seen after?
We wrap our dead in layers of onion skin.
We think about rain and if it will all hold.
Cold, encased, to stay cold,
like the snow over the graves,
how we stepped but did not walk,
to imagine him, walking from the woodpile,
always warm in the house,
stoking the fire.

There is no remedy for the ground,
for a beating as a stilled thing.

lilium, dahlia, gladiolus, narcissus, Lancaster, 2017

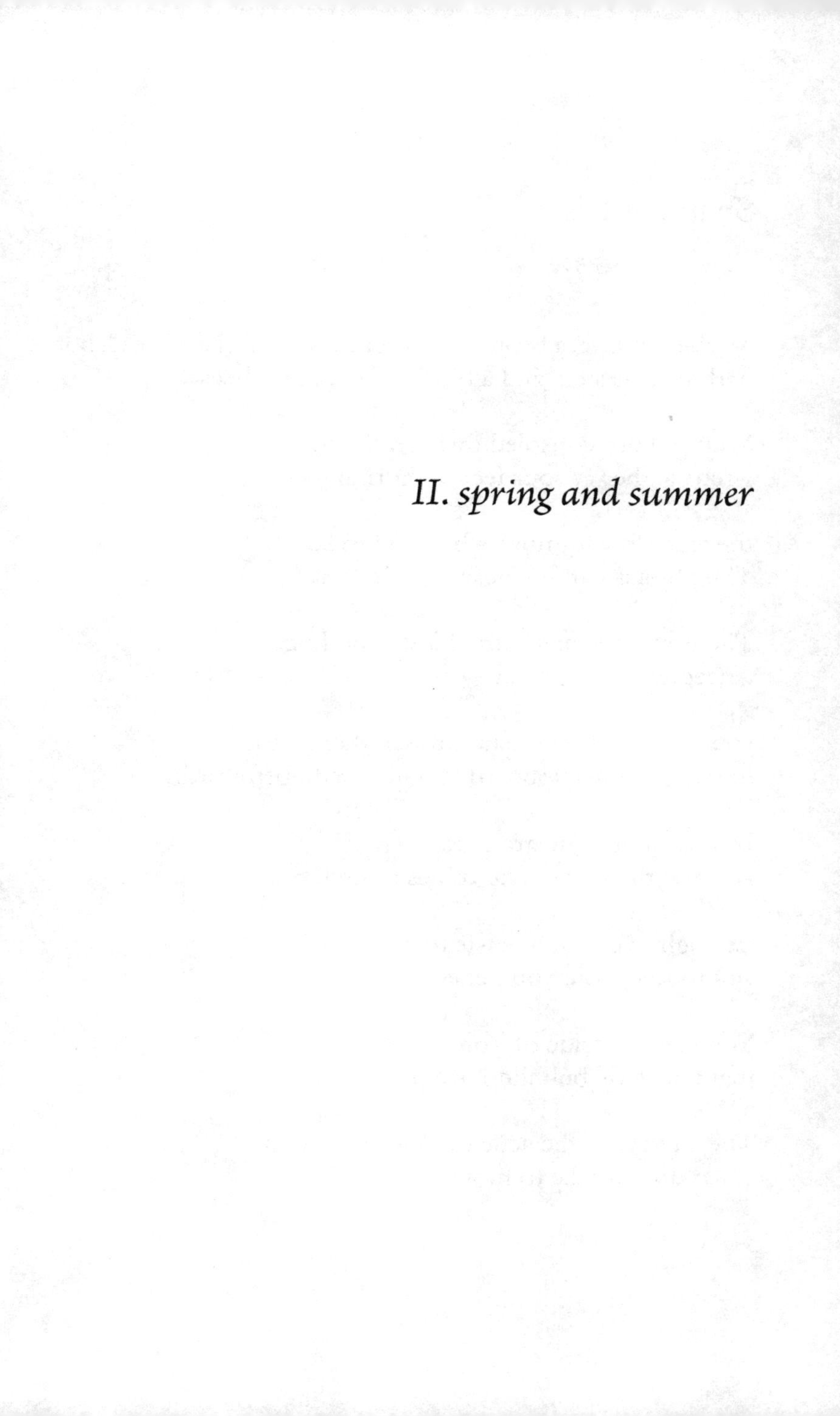

II. *spring and summer*

Shape of Iris

after Elizabeth Blackwell

Maybe a mirage: a bright orange and a slice of gingerbread, hot,
herb pie, latticed, and a block of cheddar cheese.

Your girl not consoled through the night,
wrens gather at your feet in morning—

they are slow to move when you walk.
The physics garden, near the Thames.

The way a bee meets the Flower-de-Luce,
a need to solve a need,

you transform a despair into another history,
nothing in the cupboard to a glittered northward.

If you paint pomegranates,
are they then real? The rubies glisten.

Enough river water exists to lull
you to sleep, but you persist.

You have it inside of you,
that image of bubbling over a fired crock.

The naysayers, the ache of Alexander gone.
What does it take to move rock.

The New World, undocumented
gothic rooms of flora.

It starts with the shape of iris, its petals fanning,
how you marvel at the distance, a wrinkle from across

the sea, a torn bloom to save her, what could save the child
could save the rest, could cure death from meadowed fields.

The Forest of the Suburbs

When my father dug her grave
we gathered round him to stand
near the pile of dirt under the pine.

He used his foot to force the shovel
into the earth and then it became
a simple lever and the fulcrum was

the topsoil, that land that held the rusty
base of the shovel, held his work steady
as he persisted in this world of early sun.

He had killed her, didn't mean to do it,
but she'd stayed long in the forest of the suburbs,
and having missed the sliding glass door he often

left open for her at dawn, she darted for the garage
that was closing behind his car on its way to the office,
the way it would go most Saturdays, returning

with doughnuts from the farmer's market.
And now he was burying her the way people
once buried their own dead, the way he watched

someone bury his son only ten years before.
Now he had the shovel, and the pine welcomed him,
the way all shoveling repeats in this way.

In silva, Lancaster, 1986

bluebell, harebell, witch's thimble

She has been underground as corm for long.
We touch her dirt to hear underneath.
Once a tiny potato,
what do we want to know

from her inflorescence,
her sky, her pigment heart,
downhearted, low waters,
spring ephemeral, her staying, brief,

a geophyte, storing down deep,
then each raceme, unbranched, sewn
of bellflower, their tubular corollas carpet
a forest floor, under foot, above bedrock,

above his burial in the gathered earth,
the depths, the unweathered rock, the regolith,
the eluviation, but years ago, in late April, my father
with us on the porch, above ground, we watched the blue unfold.

Hyacinthoides non-scripta

Protected by a Spine

I was your youngest daughter—you should come back for me.
It's dawn now in the valley where you walk
near a creek bed and an oak
from the first home I remember, as though transplanted
to this place beyond words, birdsong, warble.

The sage flowers from the market your oldest son bought
(or your oldest son in this world) grew full
on the nightstand at the hospice, purple, cold green.
No longer in the ground, how could they
sprout that way, Victoria Blue, *Salvia*—

impressions of *Salvia* were found
in Mt. Carmel, the Natufian period.
These were the first graves
and I wondered if this plant cleansed spirits like smudging
clears a house, burning bouquet, and so cleared a path

for you and if your spirit began to move
back and forth, as you could hardly speak,
and sometimes when you did you were a little
boy again in Brookfield, calling for your *Mama*
and couldn't always see us

surrounding you, our mother sleeping beside your bed,
those nights where we could hear your breathing even
more distinctly than before, and were you holding
firmly in this terrain like a book of beings
from the present made past, an herbarium,

or a book of beings from the past made present,
a preservation or a temporal breach—
the way a father waits to die
until he's seen all
his grown children at his bedside.

If you remove the landscape, you could
remove the forgetting,
keep the past sleeping in a book,
like pleurisy root or water arum or wild indigo,
protected by a spine—all there with you in the wind.

Walk there again on soft grass—
I remember with you and see you
leaning on the white ash tree,
its leaves almost like strawberry leaves, and you said
to dry the specimens in the newspaper

under a thick wooden board or small press,
to change the papers until no moisture remained,
to seal them with corrosive-sublimate.
To protect the specimens from moths, mold,
and mites, paint them with mercuric solution.

The poison will keep them,
those sealed fox gloves,
the way you remembered,
a held call across the meadow,
pocketed, no longer moving in the field of wild rye.

Compressio, Lancaster, 2017 and 1983; Amherst, 1845

Wangari Muta Maathai

Gone streams, gone fencing, gone midday shade,
gone soil, gone firewood, gone tamarind.

You knew not how to mend this ghosting, this breach,
the absence of the girl dreams,

what was real once, was now phantom branch,
the broad-leaved croton of your youth.

They once enveloped the land—
you knew their sound, the way the Nile

tulip trees whistled a music
through orange-spotted throats;

though this wasn't about memory, instead
the air, the way you knew breath depended

upon them, and you could mourn them,
but reached beneath mourning to bring them back.

Ghost needle weld

The Spanish needle stores
trauma in her thistle.

Morphogenetic memory
archived in the yard near the arbor.

Embroidered stitch of daisy,
a Bidens pilosa remembers

a pricked cotyledon
shred in a storm, a hail hole—

my recollection not as far
not across centuries, acres.

How could I, how did I
slip away into a thick forest?

If the world makes you forget
it's meant as a mercy, not contrition.

Amor seco knows night by last light
the far-red it sees at dusk,

tells it how long the nights
begin to become,

tells it winter is returning,
faithfully cold, the way a grief

returns in snowfall, overhead, slowly,
falling to you, finding you in the woods.

Bidens pilosa

Anna Atkins

You were the first blue
though they didn't know you.

Today curators call your work *ghostly*,
fascinated by the ammonium ferric citrate,

the potassium ferricyanide,
by that light-sensitive paper, so azure.

You walked to the edge of River Darent
that cut across North Downs, the hills afar, yet nearer.

You could be alone here with your lost mother,
plunging your arm into *Ulva latissimi*,

its ruches covering your entire hand,
as it bloomed from water.

Where did you begin and the specimen
end as you listened to the underwater forest whisper,

the way the tendrils swayed and etched themselves
into unique bodies of tangled time that remembered

and forgot at once and knew who'd gone before
and who would follow, welcoming your bone hands

into their depths and then later dried upon the cyanotypes,
their feathering within the water stilled.

Their outlines and the way they clouded the waters
could have been ghostly, but also a memory.

The way ghosts are what we'd once forgotten
and then remembered in time to see again, standing there.

Afterlives

Her hands absorb the soapy water.
It quells her foggy views through an aged
kitchen window, those night silhouettes: row of
pine, that flowering pink tree, Kwanzan
but weeping like Shidarezakura, she never learned

the name for the cherry tree without
fruit, but it looked like the two of these.
Photographs of Tokyo or the mountain,
Yoshino-Yama, covered in trees.
She could still hear one son crying in a bassinette for

milk while her oldest son lay dying
in the family room, the familiar couch,
the rust-colored, chevron afghan covered him.
The daughters looked like the blossoms near
the castle town of Hirosaki, fragile, drifting.

It was enough to still hear them all,
the way the sprinklers startled her, rain on
her sandals, the tended sidewalk, manicured
for the old robed in their dark rentals.

caelum, Lancaster

Boy, Age 7

Whereto answering, the sea,
Delaying not, hurrying not, –Whitman

When my brother swam past the buoy,
my mother raced barefooted toward the ocean.
I made castles with my pail—seagulls cried *boy*.
She could only swim out so far to reach her son.

Still my mother raced toward the ocean,
the hallway of our Colonial, dangling rotary phone—
she could only swim out so far to reach her son,
bundled in the afghan, my sister holding his hand.

The hallway of our Colonial, dangling rotary phone,
calling the doctor in the kitchen, she feared missing his death.
Bundled the last time in the afghan, my sister held his hand.
He walked without his mother through a threshold.

Calling the doctor in the kitchen, she feared missing his death.
Was his last word a command or a name for her?
He walked without his mother through a threshold.
The ferry landing, a foghorn, he wheeled his bike aboard.

Was his last word a command or a name for her?
I made castles with my pail—seagulls cried *boy*.
The ferry landing, a foghorn, he wheeled his bike aboard.
Then my brother swam past the buoy.

Puer, Lancaster, 1977

(24)

Mid-century Modern Sofa

We passed it from one to the other like a joint,
and it took up residence in dorm-like apartments
filled with Yuengling, anthologies, new flames

and late nights watching reality television over boxed
sustenance and of course boxed wine and always
boxes, belongings strewn about the temporary dwellings,

one foot in one state and the next in Florida or Colorado
or back to Pennsylvania and even California,
and the couch followed us without much fuss,

its shape slipping easily on its side against
the metal U-haul bed—
it now seemed to see all the things

our older brother never could,
gone too soon to ever leave our mother's house;
he lay on the woolen cushions all day

in his last months,
a view through the knotted pine window,
wooden arm at his back.

The wood was so heavy, solid, architectural,
impossible to carry for too long;
I couldn't understand why my mom didn't want to keep it.

It had been in the basement for years
amidst our Fisher Price and her sewing machine,
but she'd torn away by then.

The straps kept snapping and we kept
re-stapling, kneeling at its side to mend it, the way I once
knelt beside it, trying to pull my brother from sleep.

Sepal

You're holding this in a tight sepal.
Inside, the blossoms feather in bundles.
These were the days when you were all
still alive, conversations, flying a kite in sun.

If you allow the umbrella to open,
it's chartreuse and dotted with rain resting
in the foyer, and it reminds you when
your dad remembered how he once

was, when he took care of you—
you were getting married that day,
but even after the brain surgery, he
rebecame himself because you were

crying and it was storming and he told you he
would go and buy a bunch of umbrellas for
the bridesmaids, and you knew he didn't have the
money but he wanted to buy green umbrellas,

and you told him it was okay, that he didn't
need to do that, but his face looked so young
when he asked you about the umbrellas,
and even though he wouldn't dance with

you later at the wedding, but instead stayed by the bar
with random old friends of your new husband's,
you remembered the umbrellas and the way they can close
tightly like a sepal and keep the love in, even after dying.

History of Shell

We arrive wrapped in seafoam—
our ivory faces shine through bubbled lenses.
Our corpus is long lost in the Atlantic
and beyond, our ample tomb.

The Bittersweets clatter on shores:
their meat eaten in Athens,
sautéed in olive oil since antiquity.
The Red Lasaea: our tiny clam, still sleeps at highest tide,

red glass kept moist by wave splash,
her remedy for ocean life, its chill,
her umbones soaking inside
the vast brew, bottomless, passing by.

Faust, types of tellin and coquinas chime
in a small girl's pocket—mistaken for small butterflies.
The cockles aren't what once had been,
but how they seem this time.

On the wooden porch, she dusts
the sand away, soaking us
in salt-less water, blurring
the palm trees and the view East.

Cowries begin dreaming in dry terms,
scenes of ancestors and dust
rising from busy marketplaces,
bodies passed as coin, not wasted.

And in Rome, under a kerchief,
lie the remains of conch, carved in relief, a cameo.
Our souls surface as water-bailers;
we are pigment, trumpet, hoe.

Historia testae

The Skin of Willow Bark

Part the rue—evergreen,
translucent, there, always, and nowhere.
Part the knot grass—dotty pink,
carpet grass, eternity grass,
what men had stood upon,
what would coil to springs years after.
The women are there, but they are mistaken for plants,
the skin of willow bark, their arms, limbs, broken in storms.
Picture a sleeve, tattered, burlap.
Picture a basket of harvest leaves, glinting in sun.
You cannot search them easily in the forests
or meadows where they culled
among the oaken leaves and lemon balm—
they have been hidden under
hawthorn, barberry, lady's bedstraw.
You can't find them in the stacks,
the library lacking answers.
If John Gerard wanted to own a discourse
or silence recipes in the fields, quiet the motherwort,
then there wouldn't be a record of names,
instead, labels of witchery.
Instead, him transcribing by candlelight in the stolen night
the intellectual property of anonymous wise women
into *The Herball* or *Generall Historie of Plantes*.
Linnaeus named *Gerardia* after him, often root-parasitic
herbs of the snapdragon family, a name earned, remembered.
And, of course, he wasn't alone—
if he sought to institutionalize
medicine, there were others institutionalizing other things
like spells, like chants, like transubstantiation,

like holy water on skin,
and the Inquisition was "any means possible,"
the sixteenth-century church aiming
to claim healing, the spiritual,
the history of touch,
Catherine of Siena during the plague,
the way hordes of people sought
to touch the skin of a saint.

Dear One

after Rachel Carson

She could not say goodbye in Newagen
that day, imagined herself faint orange light
caught under leaves of hazel alder hedges.
And because she knew that everything was part
of everything, she did not know how souls
would ever see an end, instead transformed:
of oak, of chokecherry, of ash, of loam,
of water, beckoning, of midday storms.
When death was near, the held hours tore
apart, and quilted close to her, asleep,
but walking near the shore with Dorothy now,
the sound of spruce and ocean, tide, now neap,
the smallest rise, although the monarchs rose
so high that day—they both knew it the last.

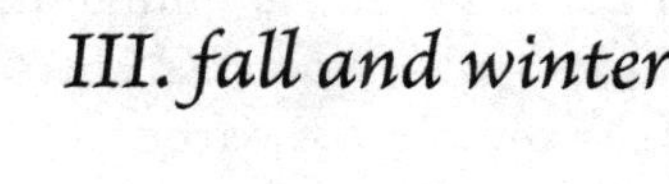

III. fall and winter

Nicotiana tabacum

Not taut like bed sheets, but hung in rows, crinkled
bundles of husk, but not husk,
leaf, large, ovate or obcordate,
egg or heart, shapes curing in the air of barns.

I admit to always finding them beautiful.
Doors wide open, as I drove
past the old red garner
many times on the way to my best friend's house.

What did we know about death, its impetus
here in our hometown,
even as my family
lived in its shadow.

Most farmers abandoned it, too much labor,
too many hands to tend it,
but the Amish could manage it
because of the large families.

Weeks of harvest are counted after topping,
when the flower is broken off,
four to five weeks for
cigar wrapper types,

four weeks for burley, cigarette filler.
Outside of Chicago, 1954:
he was eleven years old and, with his friends,
snuck through a hole in a wire

fence that surrounded the Brookfield Zoo,
scaring off rats with BB guns,
cigarettes hanging
from their mouths.

Annie Darwin's Writing Box

i.)

A way to close and open gone days inside a garden gate at Down house, near the orchard or the thinking path where her father would walk, the sand path where Annie would walk with him. Her mother took the box and added other possessions and objects, a keeping place. It could all become very small and fit inside. A way to hold them in palms, within fingertips. A thimble, a silk needle case, embroidery samples, a yellow ribbon stitched with tiny glass beads. What her hand had touched.

ii.)

Do you see her in heaven? I can see her in heaven. He couldn't see her. He saw her racing down the staircase with news for him in the morning light. *See you in the morning light.* Racing down the staircase with snuff stolen for him to enjoy in his study. Emma would open the box alone in her room. She would return to them. The surfaces began to wear away.

Condolences

It was a hot shower slowly going cold,
leaning against the stall while the water stroked
her skin and drew small continents on the flesh

of her gently bowed belly, as she guessed
what they were: the sketches read like fortune cookies.
The songs on the radio were merely directions,

prescriptions for old antibiotics in her stuffed cabinet
next to vitamins and her husband's toothpicks.
But they told her a tale like the ones of the night bird

arriving at the kitchen windowsill as she did the dishes,
stacking the pots on a yellow towel each night
while the TV and the daughters clouded up

in the family room, until all she could hear
was that black bird whispering long stories.
Could they lift her, could they show her

tempting locations: a garden of tree peonies,
flush bowing from branches, fallen heads scattered
on a pastoral path, gracefully spilled from the stem?

Was it the dream of Japan? Didn't she say
it couldn't have been a memory from a book?
It was more distant than anything distant:

usually something known, like a porch swing,
was mixed with something indescribable and sudden.
She'd later call it a biting draft, early in the morning.

Leningrad, 1938

after Akhmatova

Not Tsarskoe Selo, a familiar sleeve,
old growth, where you were a sylvan melody,
and knew names for rain in the branches, rapt or kept.

But once long ago you walked the tree-lined allées,
and in those days the willow herb would grow wild
on the path—oh kibrey, with the petals of miles and might.

And the large leaved linden her voice old,
honey, flavour, your hair unraveling:
what had you left there, near the birches and lime?

Did you think those streets would always wind round?
Isn't that the way of disappearance—sleeping children,
mother reading, then an empty chair come morning?

There is a surprise in emptiness, in a bare room;
nothing feels the same in the new world.
There is a forgotten teapot whistling through the doorways.

The North Star seems out of place.
But you were carrying elegant pavilions in your pockets.
In those hushed lines outside of central prison,

women holding loaves and notes, waiting for a glimpse,
you always knew where to find the footpath near
fruit trees, the torn-down trellis, the linden, the allée, near.

memoriam pueritia, Tsarskoe Selo, 1889-1903, Leningrad, 1938

Kitchen Ghosts

i.) The Forcing Bulb

A tight hyacinth
bulb on the kitchen
windowsill cuts
a path of color.
Fierce hand-petals
inhabit the earth.

ii.) Forced From Earth

You will see gardens
of lettuce heads,
rows of chartreuse amnesia.
Common butter produce will
now look sacred.

The vein of one leaf
is a road, and a woman
in a blue bonnet tied
at her chin
walks to the market holding
her son's small hand.

Leaf, moon, stone

Because fall was always mine,
it soon was ours.
Our walks together you called leaves, *moon,*
a yellow elm curled on its side, your hand
cupping it in your palm; it covered you,
the whole of your hand
and grew over your edges.
And you traced, tending to it, the veins, its shape.
We would save it at home, remember it
in a heavy book about planets and dust, stargazing.

Moon, like the way it all closes so tightly,
the light kept in one place, the rest starry dark.
A mooned home, watched by it overhead,
inside, sleeping mouths, just a gleam.
Just a reflection, you told me later, a stone.
But we thought it sturdy, a reliable brilliance.
A rock harnessing another light, carefully.

Now another fall, already middle school,
and I find you bereft in someone's office.
Some boys have hurt you,
you, my longing leaf, my leafing moon,
me, not a stone, me, not saving you.

Dental Records

Our boy had lost his front tooth
while I was at work and you'd saved
it for me in a white cup sitting at my desk.
Not noticing the tooth, the cup mingled
with the other dishes that night and
as we were falling asleep you asked me
about the white cup, knowing we'd forgotten
to prepare him for the tooth fairy and now
knowing that we indeed had no tooth.
I was struck by the emptying of him
down the drain, the way I spied his first
tooth as a baby and how now that tooth
was sailing somewhere without us in the water
system outside of Philadelphia.
I begged you to stop the dishwasher, dig down
into the disposal, and after, you found nothing.
Two in morning, I insisted on the P-trap,
and then, there was the tooth, cupped in your palm,
as you crouched under the sink: shining, ivory, deciduous,
milk tooth made first of embryonic cells, now calcified,
decidedly strong, made of enamel, dentin, cementum,
stronger than the garbage disposal, brilliant remains
below the earth, the way in terrible accidents
bodies can be identified by dental records.

recordari, West Chester, 2012

Dickinson walking through the woods

i.)

We were the same age when our fathers died, though living within different centuries. We should have been ready to leave them, old enough, we knew the paths, we'd memorized the walking through the woods, through the pine, where the roots rutted through, how the foliage changed seasonally. She still lived in her father's house, the Homestead, bricked and hollyhocked. The popular ochre of 1856, the house aglow. She walked the forest with Carlo, his gift to her. My childhood home a ticking projector, lost to us years earlier. My dad on a ladder painting the shutters gray. (Though ochre was his favorite color, the desk drawer of ochre pens.) A brick Colonial from 1966, the house foreclosed. Somewhere I still walk its pined edges, its forsythia abloom against the aged fence.

ii.)

Her last afternoon with her father she didn't have a "premonition" of anything being the last, but they spent time together, Viny asleep, their mother away, and her father had said he "would like it to not end." Usually she preferred to be alone, but that day in June, not knowing it his last complete day on the earth, she stayed near him, talking together in the parlor or study or even the sunlit piazza near the potted oleander. She played the piano for him, "Rest from thy loved employ." The notes are difficult to hear now (when I talked with him on the phone for the last time, both of us crying) because now they have grown into a stilled song, decibels inaudible to a body moving ahead in time, one that attempts to gather the past in a temporal nest of maple leaf.

Dickinson ambulando silvis, Amherst, 1874, Lancaster, 2017

Lancaster, A Fragment

…[the Romantic fragment is]…a remnant of something once complete and now broken or decayed… –Anne Janowitz

Above me, evenfall through
the Japanese maple leaves, a sapling,
a small tree, but not smaller than me:

a kind awning against
the chill of autumn days
that would never include him.

My hands in my Healthtex coat,
enclosure, zipper, a pocket of
acorns and stones,

sap retreating into the roots
for winter, that everything was
and would be

long afterward, grown ashes,
sproutlings undulating, farseeing
over the valley, above needle and north-grown moss.

Lancastrie, fragmentum, 1979

Linnet

Who are you, linnet; you sound similar
to songs about returning, but from where—

The Shamans call you receptacles for
the dead as though a father could fit here

inside the variegated brown under
the feathers, rusty neck, small wingspan, mere—

becoming bird to visit his daughters
in San Jose or Denver somewhere near

the coast or further east at altitude.
This brilliant capsule made for corpses arises

in apple leaves just eating rotten fruit.
If she can learn bird language, if something changes.

Lady algologist

after Margaret Gatty

Of breath, of tide, away from arms and lost
to what you meant above ground, at home.
But here, away from Ecclesfield, your mast
could bend, could tear away from birthing's tomb.
To Hastings, something bronchial brought you
to your knees—a yellow parasol
atop a field of muddled sand and weed.
And after five months away, a careful
descent into a long-forbidden sky,
apart from children, pulling at your skirt,
a circle, ache, what you no longer kept
near you, could disappear, evaporate.
The feather-arms of *Ulva linza* stole
you from the past, and left, a beach, your soul.

Penn's Woods

And at his grave
the pine grew up this way,
stories high, remnants from Penn's woods,
American larch or Eastern white pine,
seeds and soft needles for his chipmunks and the mice.

A small wren flew from one to another in another
stratosphere, and us thinking beneath the first
snow-covered ground, instead we looked above,
wondering about thresholds, the flying,
where would he choose to go,

though wanting to stay with us.
His ochre moon, the color he dreamt,
where he sat by the hedges, the bramble of mint,
his chair still there and what he looked upon,
and now those hours, anonymous hours,

the pitch pine, the larch, the hemlock,
browsed heavily by deer in deep snow.

Recordings

It was our first Christmas without him:
the floor of the living room, green shag I think, mossy
forest floor, before my mother modernized the carpeting.
We gathered cross-legged around the Panasonic,
his tape recorder, the one he carried
around playing Simon and Garfunkel.
A few brothers had yet to be born,
but the rest of us were all there.
My father, a broken MC, introduced the year,
announced the occasion, the missing son.
I think my mother held the oldest of my
younger brothers, not yet one year, on her lap.
I think we sang songs; I think we told him things,
as though by echoing into the silver microphone
our goodbyes could go traveling an unimaginable distance,
sound waves flowing through the currents of a river,
as though humans could travel on a wave to find one another.
This was patterned sound,
pleasant, predictable, the amplitude low,
the sound soft, the sound timid,
even my father's voice was hesitant
in its resignation; the energy of the wave
returned to us again and again
as we heard ourselves speak or sing and as we hit stop.

Tabulas scripto, Lancaster, December 1977

IV. spring and summer

April 1977

When he had gone, something rose high
in her chest,
or I imagined it did as we stood,

tiptoed by the window outside;
her little boy
lay on the couch wrapped in a blanket;

the maple buds still spoke singsong shine;
there were star-
flowers opening in the yard, alliums;

the doctor put a black bag over his head;
I had to look away
as my mother cried on his small body;

the bluebells under the oak parted dirt
out front: suspended,
stooped frond, weight of bells.

The Wave Machine in Oliver's Room

I'd rocked him for so many hours, nights, new moons,
even mechanized waves afford a trance.

The perigean tide abducts whatever it wants,
higher than plain spring tide, absence of tiller.

A dark moon, when closest to the earth, when
aligned with the sun, pulls everything out to sea,

a borrowed heart, only a prelude
to disappearance, a yellow shovel washed up like salvage.

I'd watch for things after a storm or the first low tide,
lime sea glass from soda in the '60s, windshields with aging

recollections of traffic, the way the rain fell, a ballad
about stepping off a grid into a tall gown of water long ago.

Underneath it was two halves of a shell—
the depths sealed away breath and worry until windows

looked the same on either side and jagged glass trailed
into substrate, a divot, and then echoes, sediment laughter.

At slack water, before the tide turned,
I sifted through driftwood,

the wrack line, wet sand, grains under my fingernails,
receiving blanket, backpack straps.

relinquens haedos, 2006 and after

(53)

Incantations

[Are we] going to progress logically and scientifically
upward or are we going to drift back to the dark ages
where witchcraft and witches reign?
–Dr. Robert Metcalf, Vice-Chancellor of the University of
California at Riverside, responding to Rachel Carson's *Silent Spring*

Wonder about sponge lace,
the holes, passages—

(it filigrees pink
inside of tidal pools)

tunnels to what isn't here,
but is here—

Think about a small thing,
its operating,

exquisite, alone, but not alone,
in need.

Bend low to peer through seaweed layers,
underneath, the winkles glim a snail world,

wet granite or something
nutbrown attached to rock,

beside white nodes of barnacle
and the lavender of mussels.

Listen to the shore,
the woodthrush, the veery,

the fields holding pockets
of weather and footstep,

and then hear at the edges and beneath the sea,
further down, plunge yourself.

Littoral, dry, and deep knitted
together with oarweed, sugar kelp, bladderwrack,

wormweed and dulse—each flutter in their own
corner of sea but also lament the dying

of each eclogue, ghosts
tapping at the window.

Home Studies in Nature

after Mary Treat, 1885

Most of the time she remained in the Pine Barrens,

her backyard in Vineland, her insect garden

surrounded by the arbor vitae hedge,

15 feet high, 150 feet in circumference.

Shrubbed domesticity, she mended

and cut back to close study:

the more I limit myself to a small area,
the more novelties and discoveries
I make in natural history

redefine the line of home and wood

…though ten miles or more through the barrens

to find *Schizaea pusilla* and other ferns and wildflowers

giant spiders   digger wasps   harvesting ants

domesticated her household the insect menagerie

even by lamplight in the arbor

if the free bird of the grove answers your call

you must be willing also   *to do his bidding*

to be without wilderness   with and within

morphed lines between inhabitants   a shared dell

an expanse   the way the wind willingly

a breath   a familiar song of trees

Forsythia

For this yellow we ran among.
For this step into the dark house, sprung lock.
For this aubade, for the earliest morning, that daybreak
that wouldn't relent, though they attempted stillness under
the covers, as though their breath had paused a long pause,
their blood had quit pulsing, but this wasn't an aubade of
lovers, intent on preserving the night, only of beloved,
the difficulty of imagining days without him, and us
the other children, the way we didn't know how
they began again, pouring milk, wiping mouths.
Called Eastertide, this weeping shrub,
who made milk sugar (so rare in a flower),
a confectionary, the lemon drops
of lament, the sting of beauty.
For this inconsistent winter that broke
open on a branch, the kind you could force,
inside in a pitcher of water, sitting in a bay window.
But that didn't need to be,
because they appeared that year, early.
The voice was only wind in their arms,
named *suspensa* for the way the branches retain light,
the way mid-air the arms could reach everywhere,
the roots no longer resting in a fixed point,
deep into soil, but alit with this hour and the past,
those hours thought gone.

Forsythia suspensa, 1978

Understory

Fist of fern unfurling
passage and stasis
simultaneous

stop motion
segment of
fiddlehead

threshold frond
we might find
what's lost

in the ledges of scree
a turning brass
doorknob

low tide line
or cloud forest
when inclined when

the switchbacks start
littoral and quiet
approach of seedpod

before your son
runs out the door
you brush his hair from his eyes

settle there sediment
find a window
intertidal song

Persephone

From what people remember now, it was spring.
And it was infectious: the laughter, the valley,
bare feet on fresh grass, the girls with baskets, thatched,
ready to bring their mothers home violets,
perfume of hyacinth, drifting.

Though the taxonomy of the flowers
varies in every telling, a grove
of white lilies, those that appear
at funerals or Roman orchids which grow in Greece
in March, early April—these all could be a dream

and now she wonders what was and wasn't
true about that day before the summer solstice
which wasn't named yet by her mother, just a day,
when all the days gleamed like porcelain,
cool to touch, her last morning in the kitchen,
breakfast of *teganitai* and honey.

But one thing is certain to her, certain to her mother—
this is the story of a child
and a story of grief—
she had found the perfect narcissus.
Though all daffodils, fluted and belled,

possess a perfection, this one was otherworldly
and to a child such an excitement rises up,
and when she picked it, its roots gave way;
beneath the flowers flew spirits;
the earth cracked in two; everything
below the buds shook open.

Even though the story became
a palimpsest, still, the abduction, the rape couldn't
be written over and some versions
claim she couldn't forgive herself,
some claim there wasn't a crime,
there wasn't Hades carrying her off,

then on top of her, forcing himself.
This is also familiar for she was a child
on her way home, but rewritten as a woman.
And her mother's search across Athens,
frantic and named hysterical after her womb's
name, while it sat empty inside of her,

her sandals tramped through miles
of pasture, mud up to her knees
until she knew the truth and wept
with grief making the months colder.
You see she wasn't bitter—
she didn't mean to punish the summering.
Reading under the olive trees.
Night strolls through the jasmine.

Yet the cold still got to her, through her clothes
as though she felt the window always at her neck—
and even though now, after she named it long ago,
we think of winter as a chance to burrow against
the fright, inside candlelit, a teacup, but
then it was new and a consequence of a woman
feeling something in her bones.

Late August

Why do you keep trying to stop it?
The limbs keep growing,
the faces changing, the small hands

you forgot to mold in white clay
like the other
mothers did so long ago before

the strollers were given away.
Each year you must
say goodbye to the particulars

of endearment like shapes we see
in the dark
after our eyes have adjusted: radio

songs that you all knew the words to,
sundresses now
too small, her yodel from the top

of the staircase, rituals of dishes,
or the novels
they read so quickly with the light

on in the hallway, rapt in their beds,
whispering
make believe games that you wait

for them to stop playing ever
again.
But right now the crickets are here.

nuper Augusta

Cashel 1995

We were here before, weren't we?
You lay in bed in the dark and remember us
remembering the hills and green, so greenly.
It was so holy beyond the ruins,
farther than the eye,
(Forget the nettle
and the stream.
My hand in the rill and
only the farmer believing me.)
as far as we could see, and more, but not
a wine-dark sea, not godly.
Because of the hazy distance,
it couldn't go on forever
but was everywhere, and now
as your children rustle,
and the dishwasher song stirs,
it is the sward you see
on the dark ceiling,
us, there, seen.

Jane Colden below the guardrail

Driving on I-84 toward Newburgh,
toward Coldengham, passing a swamp
that once stretched over this highway,

Andromeda blooming over a median, bog
rosemary, those petals of needlepoint pink
flocking an exit ramp or *Erythronium*, Dog's

Tooth, blue leaves stalking a yield sign, this gutted
marshland, gleaned, macadam poured into its crevices.
But then I see you, the way ghosts are seen:

through layers of light,
the way your clothing overlaps, veiling—
the haze of a stayer made of whale bone,

then the stomacher stitched and hooked,
a hooped petticoat, lace apron, the kerchief across
your shoulders, sun on your neck, basket at your wrist.

Your story is buried under the highway.
So many do not know your yellowing,
that mourn of a lullaby in a dark room,

as though you sang them to sleep,
the Marsh Marygold towering from wet meadows.
You saved your father and he chose you

to save him—too old to walk the woods and wetlands,
still he wanted the plants to transform him,
not an alchemy, but a discovery, a commendation

from the botanical intelligentsia,
for finding species in the wilderness.
At first you stayed fenced in your mother's garden,

drew only the common dandelion,
the outline of the hollyhock;
then something grabbed hold of you.

You tied your bonnet early that morning
and went out in search of the wildings,
because he needed you and because their arms

began to draw nearer.
The more you walked out into the 3000 acres,
the more you wondered, how easily you could speak

with them, each bore a pearling,
something most of us believed
we had lost so many years ago,

that radiant psalm that could calm and stir,
mitigate a field, grasses in wind, and you saw
them this way: the polygala, the penniroyal, the wake-robin.

You took each one carefully in your hands,
your sight, your acuity made the flora a-flight,
in the stale manor, pocketed shutters swung open.

Umbra, Newburgh, 2018 and 1753

The Wave Machine in Ingrid's Room

The way she sleeps or doesn't sleep
depends on the moon,
how it pulls so hard at the sea sometimes—
not a neap tide, but a spring tide, when all the orbs align.

We drift to the seabed
with the plankton, primordial material, volcanic ash,
and weathered rocks, and the underwater
breathes in our ears, the sun quivers through
the blue, and here I'm the grown girl

in the bandeau again, before the babies,
and now falling in the sea always meant for me,
where every last one will convene.
There's my calculus teacher with the ponytail
who built the solar system out of a bed sheet,
a projector, and a wooden half-sphere.

There are three of my grandparents
walking together on the ocean floor:
one couple is showing my grandpa
where everything is, where to mail things.
And there's my older brother, still a little boy,
not much older than my son,
just like the photo near Orlando.

He's waving; he's sad to see me grown,
at first mistakes me for my mother,
but I'm older now than she was,
just a stranger really, trying to swim

near him, the water swirling, the gravity
reminding both of us how
little it matters what we wish.
I want to show him Ingrid, but not here—

she looks so much like he'd remember.
And we both know that it's too late;
he's missed everything,
and I'm unknown to him.
So I swim closer, as much as I can
against the undertow,
and he signals me back toward the surface,
a mime in the Caribbean thrashing
at me like an older brother,

but I can't move, can't imagine
leaving him again,
and then he takes my foot
like we did at the bottom
of the sky-blue painted pool
and hoists me up through the water like a porpoise.

Ghost pipe, ghost plant, corpse plant
(1886 and backwards)

In those days, it was easier to walk into the shadow of the forest. An emptier place, our hiddenness held more tightly, *Matryoshka*. She found the base of the Douglas Fir because she wanted a threshold in Amherst. She needed to reach a kind of boundary. This is now a rare occurrence. To find a threshold of pine needles and to see us bowing back down to the dirt, anemic and crystal and jelly and albino and amnesia green. We don't depend on light. We are understory. We are of the depths of the forest, of rot. Not the foliage, not stems of beginnings, but what is forgotten. Yet if you find us, if you find the littoral line of needles, the translucent color of growth and decay, what trembles between, the dreams of *Monotrope uniflora*, then we move from your periphery. Those gone, those once out of focus, are now seen. They were there all along.

Ghost pipe, ghost plant, corpse plant
(1886 and before)

It is a complicated relationship. We are more than
parasitic. There is a symbiotic association. The fungi host
us, but it is a mycorrhiza and has another relationship
with a vascular host plant, its roots. More than this, it is
the mycelium. Thread-like white, invisible, stretching for
miles; akin to whispering in a dark room when you think
you see a figure and you figure it's dark adaptation, that
adjustment of the retina or your tendency to startle easily.
There is another seeing. That is the way anyone navigates
between two worlds.

She called nature a haunted house, the forest, needled
path, under the fir. We were ghostly in that our roots
witnessed. We kept coming back across centuries; we
lived a religion. A terrestrial afterlife in the shadow of the forest.

Taraxacum

A star, cold
feather arms
folded on itself
and onto all it
happens upon

Beyond the first field
it knows it grows
more in the unknown
but also knows
it will diminish
its first heart

Ghost garden

Grasmere Journals, 1800-1803

She blurred a home within the Lake Country, each edge
fogged, the line of lamp-post moss, winding here and
there. Dorothy and Mary took "candlelight into the
garden" watching the brooms bloom. She wrote a way to
live among the scent-less violets and hackberry, the crab
and crowfoot. The everyday rituals of baked bread or an
evening walk to the waterfall at twilight with an armful of
lemon thyme carried home and planted, home and wood
and garden all out of focus, presbyopia. Each moored to
another. The garden at Dove Cottage like the junctions
in the azalea tufted with pincushion moss at the bends.
An adaptor. The topography of intimacy, the garden
walls, she planted London's pride upon it, long before
the Blitz when the groundcover bloomed upon bomb
sites, growing well over neglected earth, constructing a
garden in its proliferation. The breaches in the wall, a
missing stone, a viewfinder, extending across hill-tops,
sheep tracks, the stream murmuring. She searched
cloverleaf, those exchanges, a biocentric convocation,
the way everything meant something to everything else.

Lantana

In a dream you were reading an email about a ghost
that someone had seen in the woods
near a grove of wildflowers,
and then suddenly your father appeared
at a patisserie with your mother,
and the three of you stared at the glass case:

croissant, éclair, macarons of raspberry,
lavender, and lime, all in straight rows
shimmering at the three of you.
Your father said how delicious everything looked
and you knew he loved dessert, one of the last

things he had eaten, and you asked
if he'd want to share something,
and he made a face that looked like
he was afraid to break some news, and he asked if
he had to, knowing that he couldn't anymore

in his world, and you understood
and smiled holding his arm to be sure
he was real, making sure he stayed
in the sunlight of the cafe-lined streets, the reflection
against the shop window, and he said he knew

how sad you were this winter, and he had visited you
to make sure, and you knew he was right
about the sadness and then you had to bring
your mother closer because she was slipping away
in the dream, still in her flowered bathrobe stitched

on white terry, but when you motioned her back he had
disappeared and then you and your mother
walked together in a grove of candy-colored flowers,
lantana, that grew outside
of your house years ago in Florida, always dream-like.

Herbarium

We did and didn't know those days of peat
and early summer rain, fresh mulch humid
in garden beds as we unhinged the gate
to meander unrooted, meadow's hood.
We hid in rye grass, years of rue shadows.
You have gone now it seems—to cobalt clouds;
we forgot more than we thought—maple leaves,
a canopy, your green MG, the sound
of branches, fog, our voices through the hallways,
yard roses, shade of oak, the weeds beneath
our feet, of puddles, wasps, macadam steams.
Impatiens pink in baskets drip and we
watch a youthful picture show, a ticking
projector, what we didn't know would break.

Culling Stone

Days dressed in the weaves of the creek,
the current sifts me, tied in sleep.

Slips of water whirl me deep
into sediment laced with wisps that keep

time against knotted chest of bottom, smooth
stream, the echoes that soothe

the boy's feet before he snags me
from bed into fist, an egg of milk, like plenty.

My body shades the rills and reaches of his palm;
instead of a toss across the bank, he holds calm.

Moss

Until the Moss had reached our lips
And covered up—Our names— –ED

Where are you in the woodland—
if you reside against an elm,

small, herbaceous, coiling and keeping,
an earnest supposition to persist

amidst the weathering, to cling
to rock, a steady preposition: to,

as in indebted or grateful or toward
something, what is not yet found,

an amorous proposition for blooming, for spores,
to remaining in spite of the vanishings,

a provider of habitats for algae and small animals
or the creation of the amenable, the conditions

of soil for other plants, held water
for the humidity of entire habitats.

Always there remains somewhere beneath,
where you always are, oh bryophyte,

somewhere inmost, a place we haven't
returned or turned over,

as though in Arden,
a forest capable of hiding

a generation, quietly
in the thick, lost,

reminding us, that which is still,
is not gone.

Diatoms

*[Common in the Rehoboth Bay these microscopic plants are] intricately
sculptured with pits, pores, spines, ribs, and spindles. The ones most common
in these waters are like tiny glass houses linked together in a train.* –Jennifer
Ackerman

*Everything tends to make us believe that there exists a certain point of the
mind at which life and death, the real and the imagined, past and future,
the communicable and incommunicable, high and low, cease to be perceived as
contradictions.* –André Breton

You sleep in the wing feathers of diving seabirds.
You are nowhere but live everywhere,
your existence some kind of metaphor for god.
Upon grains of sand you grow a lemon grove.
Oh, we walked through the grove so long ago.
My hands, my fingertips, cannot hold you.
What is the difference between a dream sequence
and something microscopic? Blurred lines or sunspots.
Instead of reality you conjure finality, funeral clothes,
closing the door of a sold house, the day
I last walked the halls of the walkup from 1924.
At the beginning of time you grew wilder,
you, the smallest of plants, the miniature wood,
but human nature interceded, the angling
Anthropocene, the contribution of my species.
I could have contributed to your life—I could
have been a memory on your deathbed.
I should not hold you, should not disturb
your work here but still yearn to know you.
Leave no trace. Leave no trace of you.

Your arrival long before mine and my
inability, the way my naked eyes
cannot see, promises something strange to my heart.
We don't need to know everything in this earthen place,
but I would like to imagine that your glass
houses reside with souls of those presumed
unreachable, gone from the world, as though
if we just used our readers, focused a bit harder
in the dying light, then we could see their faces again.

Cymatosira belgica and other species, Lewes, DE 2021

petrichor

The milieu after rain,
we walk into it unencumbered.

Ancients thought a heaven
lived inside this dry ground.

What rises is a return or our returning,
who left and who came back?

Those we have loved and buried
or our forgotten past deep inside a seed.

Notes

Shape of Iris

When her husband was sent to debtor's prison and she and her daughter fell into poverty, Elizabeth Blackwell utilized her art training to document plants from the New World and support her family. In 1737, Blackwell published *A Curious Herbal : Containing Five Hundred Cuts of the Most Useful Plants Which Are Now Used in the Practice of Physick*. Doctors and herbalists, including those of the Royal College of Physicians, celebrated her work for years after.

Wangari Muta Maathai

The first African woman and environmentalist to earn the Nobel Peace Prize, and the first woman in East and Central Africa to earn a PhD, Maathai began the Green Belt Movement in Kenya as a response to clearcutting, first practiced by the British imperialists to build tea plantations. The movement allowed local women to plant trees for wages. To date, over 30 million trees have been planted across Africa thanks to her efforts.

Anna Atkins

Atkins, a botanist and photographer, was considered the first person to illustrate a book with photographs, *Photographs of British Algae* (1849-1850), and the first woman to take a photograph. She signed her work AA and some thought this stood for Anonymous Amateur, which hid her identity for a time.

The Skin of Willow Bark

In England, in order to avoid "sorceries, witchcrafte, and other inconveniencies," a law was enacted in 1512 against any medical practice not licensed by a body of surgeons or physicians. Unlicensed women were later allowed to practice, but not for profit or survival, for charity only. Many now believe this allowed the establishment to gain ownership of the medicines created by wise women for the poor.

Dear One

The poem chronicles a letter Rachel Carson wrote to Dorothy Freeman in September 1963, shortly after Carson delivered testimony to JFK's Science Advisory Committee on the dangers of pesticides. She died of breast cancer in the spring of 1964.

Nicotiana tabacum

Tobacco was the largest cash crop in Lancaster County from the mid-nineteenth century to the early twenty-first.

Annie Darwin's Writing Box

It is believed that the Darwins' oldest daughter died of tuberculosis soon after her tenth birthday.

Lady algologist

Margaret Gatty would later publish *British Seaweeds* in 1862.

Home Studies in Nature

Mary Treat, naturalist and periodic correspondent with—and teacher to—Darwin, published *Home Studies in Nature* in 1885. Excerpts from the book are included in the poem.

Jane Colden below the guardrail

Colden was the first woman botanist in America and her *Botanic Manuscript* was the most comprehensive description of flora from the region written by anyone before the nineteenth century. She abandoned her botanical work in her thirties, when she married Dr. William Farquhar. Only seven years later, she died in childbirth, the baby dying days after.

American, eighteenth-century spellings of plant names come directly from *Botanic Manuscript of Jane Colden*.

Herbarium Notation

Some of the poems in this book are concluded with data or "labels."
Historically and even today, herbaria rely on these varied and dynamic
labels, each specimen often receiving its Latin name, the date, place, and
the altitude of its discovery, as well as brief descriptions and specific,
special habitat conditions.

Acknowledgements

Thanks to the editors who first published these poems.

Boxcar Poetry Review: "Mid-century Modern Sofa"

Cider Press Review: "Anna Atkins"

Cordella: "Herbarium"

Gold Wake Live: "The Wave Machine in Oliver's Room" and "lilies, dahlias, gladioli, daffodils"

Josephine Quarterly: "Understory"

Mid-American Review: "Dental Records"

Subtropics: "History of Shell"

The Bennington Review: "bluebell, harebell, witch's thimble"

The Buddhist Poetry Review: "Condolences"

2River View: "Afterlives"

These poems appeared in *The Forest of the Suburbs,* a chapbook, (Five Oaks Press, 2015): "The Forest of the Suburbs," "History of Shell," "Culling Stone"

I have great gratitude for the support of my teachers and friends who have been readers and editors along the way, including Robin Becker, Karen Fish, Graham Foust, C.S. Giscombe, Michael Hofmann, Sarah Kugel, William Logan, Christopher Merkner, Bin Ramke, Selah Saterstrom, Spring Ulmer, Sidney Wade, Lauren Wilcox, and Eliot Khalil Wilson.

I am also grateful for the research and writing of historians, herbalists, botanists, scientists, biographers, scholars, poets, and artists, including Emily Dickinson, Mary Treat, Wangari Muta Maathai, Dorothy Wordsworth, Rebecca Laroche, Jane Colden, Cadwallader Colden,

Rachel Carson, William Souder, Elizabeth Blackwell, Linda Lear, Jennifer Ackerman, Annie Darwin, Charles Darwin, Ruth Padel, Margaret Gatty, Anna Akhmatova, Anna Atkins, Seymour Schwartz, Richard B. Sewall, Terry Gifford, Sara Stidstone Gronim, Luce Irigaray, and those unnamed.

All of my appreciation to my editor, Bridgette Brados, David Pischke, Heather Lang-Cassera, Risa Pappas, and everyone at Tolsun Books for the support of this book.

Author photo by Sloan Blanton

Molly Kugel is the author of the chapbooks *The Forest of the Suburbs* (Five Oaks, 2015) and *fo gheasaibh: poems of Rachel Carson* (dancing girl press, forthcoming 2022). Her poems have appeared most recently in *Bennington Review*, *Calyx*, *Josephine Quarterly*, *Mid-American Review*, and *Cider Press Review*. She recently completed her PhD in Literary Studies at the University of Denver, and she is the Ecology Editor for *Cordella Magazine*.

CPSIA information can be obtained
at www.ICGtesting.com
Printed in the USA
JSHW061140090722
27779JS00003B/231